The New Rules of Dating

A Christian Guide for Navigating the Complex World of Dating Today

Joy Ani

The New Rules of Dating

Copyright © 2024 Joy Ani

The moral right of the author has been asserted in accordance with the copyright Designs and Patent Act 1988.

First published 2024

ISBN: 978-1-916667-06-8

Published by:

Joy of Many Generations
info@joyofmanygenerations.com
Telephone: +44 (0) 7914 945 246
www.joyofmanygenerations.com

Unless otherwise noted, all scriptures are from the HOLY BIBLE, NEW INTERNATIONAL VERSION ®. Copyright© 1973, 1978, 1984, 2011 by Biblica, Inc.™. Used by permission of Zondervan.

All rights reserved. No part of this book may be reproduced in any form or by any electronic or mechanical means, including information storage and retrieval systems without permission in writing, from the publisher.

DISCLAIMER

While the stories within this book may draw inspiration from real-life experiences, the author has taken creative liberties to write them. Names have been changed to protect the privacy of those who may have inspired the characters. Any resemblance to actual persons, living or dead, or actual events is purely coincidental.

Contents

Reviews...viii
Dedication xiii
Acknowledgement xiv
Foreword.. xv
Introduction... 1
Chapter 1 3
Navigating the New Realities of the Dating World 3

> The State of Dating in Today's Society....................3
> The Evolution of Dating Rules 4
> Online Dating: Risks and Benefits...........................8
>
>> Risks of online dating 8
>> Benefits of Online Dating...................................9
>> Note of Caution 11
>
> Exploring the Changing Dynamics of Gender Roles: A Biblical Perspective..12
> Beyond Casual Sex: The Risks of Hookup Culture for Christians...15

Chapter 2 19
The Foundations of Christian Dating 19

What the Bible Says About Dating and Relationships
.... 19
Understanding God's Plan for Marriage 22
The Role of Prayer in Christian Dating 24
Role And Influence Of Parent In Dating Choices. 28

Chapter 3 31
Preparing for Dating... 31

Self-Discovery: Building Self-Worth and Personal Growth 31
Identifying and Addressing Emotional Baggage .. 34
Family and Culture: Balancing Expectations in Relationships.. 37

Chapter 4 41
Building Healthy Relationships 41

Balancing Individual Needs and Relationship Goals in Christian Dating.. 41
The Role of Compatibility in a Successful Christian Relationship 43
The Power of Communication in Christian Dating 46
Understanding Consent and Boundaries in Christian Dating 49

Red Flags and Warning Signs in Christian Relationships 51
Conflict Resolution and Forgiveness in Christian Relationships 54

Chapter 5 57
Navigating Breakups and Rejection 57

How to handle rejection and breakups in a healthy way 57

    Focus on self-care 58
    Seek God's Wisdom and Direction 58
    Don't play the blame game 59
    Allow Yourself to Grieve 59
    Practice Forgiveness 60
    Find Support from Your Community 60
    Don't make hasty decisions 60
    Don't rush it 61

Finding hope and healing after heartbreak 61

    Stay Positive 62
    Seek God's Guidance and Comfort 62
    Seek for professional help 63

Chapter 6 65
Personalized Stories About Dating 65

Real-life dating experiences shared by Christian parents and young adults 65

A Journey to Finding Love Through Faith 66
Finding Love Online: A Christian's Journey..... 67
Choosing Faith Over Love 68
From Heartbreak to Happily Ever After 70

Lessons learned from these experiences 71
Locating God's word for difficult situation 73

Chapter 7 .... **77**
Maintaining Purity and Intimacy in Christian Dating **77**

Overcoming societal pressure to be in a relationship
.... 77
Understanding God's Plan for Sexual Purity 79
Mastering Physical Desires and Setting Healthy Boundaries in Dating 81
The benefits of accountability and community..... 86
Building Emotional Intimacy and Connection 87

Chapter 8 .... **91**
Preparing for Marriage **91**

Discerning God's Will in Your Relationship......... 91
Understanding the Purpose of Engagement and courtship 95
Premarital Counselling: Setting Your Marriage Up for Success 98

What is Premarital Counselling? 98

Chapter 9 102
Answering Common Questions About Dating 102

What is the Purpose of Dating? 102

How Do I Know if This Person is the One? ... 103
How do I Find a Godly Partner? 106
How do I navigate Cultural Differences in Dating? 107
How do I handle disagreements with my partner in a Godly way? 110
How do I overcome past relationship baggage or trauma in order to have a healthy dating experience? 113

Conclusion 118

Final thoughts and words of wisdom 119

Bibliography 122

REVIEWS FOR THE BOOK

Congratulations to you, Joy Ani. You are an exceptional writer. I believe this book will help many enjoy the best of their relationship.

"New Rules for Dating" brings a Christian perspective to the often challenging areas of modern romance. By weaving biblical principles into the scene of dating and advice, the book offers a unique and faith-centred approach to relationships. It provides guidance on honouring values, practicing patience, and building genuine connections grounded in shared beliefs in the pursuit of love with spiritual principles, making the book a valuable resource for those seeking a fulfilling relationship and a steadfast commitment to their faith.

Personally, I love to highlight these topics within the pages of the book. 'Maintaining Purity and Intimacy in Christian Dating' and 'Preparing for Marriage' are crucial aspects. This is the missing ingredient in the modern dating world. Many have lost touch with values, sense of purpose and purity. By delving into these topics, the book provides readers with practical insights into driving the delicate balance between promoting emotional intimacy and upholding Christian values. It uniquely equips readers with guidance on setting boundaries, and communication strategies.

New Dating Rules not only addresses the unique challenges faced by Christian singles but also empowers them to approach dating with a strong foundation rooted in faith.

I am grateful for the chance to explore this book. As an author who specializes in relationships and a certified marriage counsellor, I've gained significant insight reading through this book. I wholeheartedly recommend this as a must-read. The depth of values and knowledge within is truly commendable.

Rev. Doreen Kattah
Author, Keeping the Love Alive

* * *

Reviews for the Book

Wow! Amazing! Great read! These were the words I could express from reading such a timely needed book. There are a lot of failing relationships these days especially among the Christian community which needs to be checked.

"The New Rules of Dating" is not your regular romantic or relationship book. It really gives you real lifetime experiences and solutions to unattended problems in relationships.

I could easily connect with most of the experiences and I must say it is a must read for singles, young couples, counsellors, pastors and those desirous of having a great relationship.

What is intriguing about this book is the highlighted need for keeping your values and faith which I believe are very necessary to having a very peaceful and loving relationship. Our walk in this world is by faith, your faith must be strengthened and you need to uphold your values to have a great life.

Another highlighted topic to really consider is 'emotional baggage'. This is one of the things that destroy people and relationships, and should be given the needed attention. A lot of youth especially young ladies are really carrying such baggage which must be offloaded for them to experience true love and happiness.

Pastor Benedicta Nartey
CEO/Founder - Benekie Foundation

* * *

I would like to congratulate Pastor Joy Ani for writing 'The New Rules Of Christian Dating'. The Spirit of God continues to direct the sons and daughters of God regarding living a holy and righteous life. Pastor Joy has undoubtedly provided these nuggets of biblical truths that will help readers make the right choices and identify possible red flags while dating. This book has been written in a season when young adults seeking to have Godly relationships are in a real dilemma.

New Rules Of Christian Dating gives meaningful insights into dating in today's world. The book offers key guidance to responsible dating and most importantly having God at the center of the journey. A lot of young Christians preparing for dating in this generation are not immune to the challenges, pressures, and influence of social media and internet dating. Lack of knowledge of the dangers out there in the world has led some heartbroken and disappointed. Penning this insightful book, the author guides the reader to consider the importance of possessing certain qualities such as honouring God, self-worth, maturity, and personal development before dating.

The concept running through this Christian guide for navigating the complex world of dating today is to empower the reader to be mindful of the dangers of falling out of the will of God but at the same time enjoy the pleasantness in meeting and dating someone who shares same values and principles of Christian relationship.

This guide to navigating dating today has rich biblical resources and God-given counsel. I strongly recommend this book to anyone seeking to embark on dating with the intention of marriage in the future.

Rev. Margaret Maccarthy
Author, Marriage Spices

DEDICATION

To those yearning for a love story penned by faith,
not fate.

ACKNOWLEDGEMENT

My deepest gratitude goes to all who played a part in bringing this book to life and also to God the almighty for the inspiration and privilege. To Marcia Dixon for the foreword, Rev. Doreen Kattah, Pastor Benedicta Nartey and Rev. Margaret Maccarthy for the reviews, and to the other brave individuals who shared their personal stories; thank you for trusting me with your vulnerabilities and enriching this book with your truths. And most of all, to the readers who pick up this book, thank you for embarking on this journey with me. May you find guidance, hope, and inspiration within these pages.

FOREWORD

Dating, finding the one and building a successful marriage, even for Christians, has become a difficult and complicated exercise in our modern world.

The issue is not just who to date as Christians, but how to date, and during the dating stage, understanding what qualities to look for in a potential spouse, and if they find a spouse, how to prepare for marriage – all the while being a good example to others.

In this much needed book, The New Rules of Dating: A Christian guide for navigating the complex world of dating today, Joy Ani provides a step-by-step guide on how Christians should conduct themselves whilst looking for a spouse.

There're useful chapters on dating, preparing oneself mentally to date, guidance on how to retain one's Christian principles whilst dating, how to build healthy relationships, coping with rejection and relationship break-ups, maintaining one's sexual purity, and marriage preparation.

With so much confusion around Christian dating, courting and marriage these days, partly due to worldly influence, this book serves as a welcome reminder that God's word provides guidance and inspiration believers can apply to all aspects of their lives – including the search for a lifelong partner.

What readers will find particularly helpful about The New Rules of Dating is the inclusion of real-life dating experiences of Christians which adds that touch of realism and highlights how applying scripture impacts one's dating experiences.

The New Rules of Dating: A Christian guide for navigating the complex world of dating today is a book that individuals on the dating journey will find useful and is also a must have for anyone who provides Christian teaching on dating, courting and marriage. Enjoy.

Marcia Dixon MBE
Editor, Black Christian and Single
Editor/Publisher: Keep the Faith magazine
www.keepthefaith.co.uk

INTRODUCTION

It's no secret that we live in a world where relationships and dating have become more complicated than ever before. With the advent of dating apps and the rise of hook-up culture, it can be difficult to know how to navigate the dating scene as a Christian.

In this book, "The New Rules of Dating," we'll explore the latest trends and challenges facing Christians in the modern dating world. We'll delve deep into the biblical principles that should guide our approach to relationships and discover how to build a strong foundation for a Christ-centred relationship.

You'll discover the importance of cultivating qualities like patience, integrity, and self-control, as well as the value of knowing your own worth and staying true to your values. With practical advice and real-life stories, you'll learn how to navigate the complex world of dating with confidence and grace.

We'll also delve into the importance of Christian values and principles in dating, including honesty, integrity, and sexual purity. You'll learn how to set healthy boundaries, recognize red flags, and build trust and intimacy with your partner.

If you're tired of the endless cycle of swiping, texting, and ghosting, and ready to pursue a relationship that honours God and brings you joy, then "The New Rules of Dating" is the guide you've been waiting for. Let us together explore the new rules of dating that are essential to building a life-giving relationship that honours God and brings joy and fulfilment to our lives.

Chapter 1

NAVIGATING THE NEW REALITIES OF THE DATING WORLD

The State of Dating in Today's Society

In today's society, the landscape of dating has shifted dramatically. It is now often characterised by casual hook-ups, one-night stands, and a lack of commitment. But for those of us who value traditional relationships and are looking for something deeper and more meaningful, this can be disheartening.

It can be tempting to follow the crowd and engage in casual relationships, but you must remember that your values should always come first. This new trend should not be a reason to abandon your values and principles in the quest for love.

With the rise of social media and dating apps, it can be difficult to build genuine connections with people and to find someone who shares your values and beliefs. But the good news is that with God's help, the journey towards discovering a genuine relationship that aligns with your values is still achievable.

As you navigate this new landscape of dating, you must recognise that your approach to dating and relationships must align with your purpose and destiny. Your focus should always be on God and His plan for your life. You must trust that He will guide you to the right person at the right time and that your relationship will be a testament to His love and grace.

The Evolution of Dating Rules

The traditional dating rules that once governed courtship have largely fallen by the wayside in today's society. The world may tell you that traditional dating rules are outdated and no longer relevant, but this couldn't be further from the truth. In fact, it is more important than ever to have a strong sense of what you believe and to be intentional about seeking out relationships that align with those beliefs.

Here are some reasons why traditional dating rules are no longer relevant:

- *Technology has changed the way we date:* With the rise of dating apps and social media, traditional dating rules have become outdated. People are meeting online, swiping left or right, and building relationships through digital communication.

- *Gender roles have evolved:* Traditional dating rules were often based on rigid gender roles, with men expected to take the lead and women expected to be passive. But as society has become more egalitarian, these roles have evolved, and women are now taking more initiatives in the dating space.

- *Casual dating is more common:* In the past, dating was often seen as a precursor to marriage. But today, many people are more interested in casual dating or just having fun. Many people view relationships as disposable, something to be discarded when they no longer serve their needs or desires. This mindset runs counter to the biblical view of relationships, which emphasizes the importance of covenantal commitment and selfless love.

- ***Individualism is valued more highly:*** In today's society, people are encouraged to be themselves and follow their own path. Traditional dating rules may feel too prescriptive or restrictive for those who value their independence.

- ***Diversity is celebrated:*** Traditional dating rules often had a narrow view of what constituted a "normal" relationship. But today, people from all walks of life are dating and forming relationships. Traditional rules may not apply to the wide range of relationships that exist today.

However, as a Christian, you must recognize that the culture in which you live has a powerful influence on you. It is all too easy to fall into the trap of thinking that traditional dating rules are no longer relevant or important. You may be tempted to go along with the prevailing attitudes and behaviours of your peers, even if they do not align with your beliefs.

But the truth is that you are called to be set apart from the world. You are called to live lives that are characterized by holiness, righteousness, and obedience to God's will. This means that you cannot simply go along with the flow of culture when it comes to relationships and dating. You must approach these matters with intentionality and discernment, seeking God's guidance every step of the way.

While traditional dating rules may seem to no longer be relevant, there are still some basic biblical principles that can guide us in building healthy relationships. Dating rules such as abstaining from sex until marriage and setting clear expectations for communication and commitment are still just as important today as they were in the past.

Beyond being bound by the rules and traditions of the world, we should rather be guided by the principles of God's word.

Online Dating: Risks and Benefits

As a Christian, you are called to honour God in all aspects of your life, including your dating relationships. However, in a world where online dating and social media are common places, it might be difficult to navigate the dating scene while staying true to your Christian values. The internet offers a vast array of opportunities to connect with new people, but it also presents risks that you should be aware of.

Risks of online dating

One of the risks of online dating is the temptation to compromise your standards in order to find a partner. It's easy to get caught up in the excitement of meeting new people and overlook potential red flags or warning signs. As a Christian, you should approach online dating with a prayerful and discerning mindset, seeking God's guidance in your search for a partner. Don't let the excitement of meeting new people lead you astray from what truly matters: honouring God in all aspects of your life, including your relationships.

Social media can be a breeding ground for comparison and jealousy, leading to unhealthy dynamics in our relationships. You may find yourself constantly comparing your own relationships to those you see on social media, leading to feelings of inadequacy or insecurity. It's important to remember that what people post online is often a carefully curated version of their lives, and you should not base your own worth or relationship satisfaction on these idealised images.

The anonymity of the internet can make it easier for people to deceive and misrepresent themselves. You should strive to be truthful and transparent in your online interactions and avoid engaging in behaviours that compromise your integrity.

Engaging in online dating and social media can also be addictive and time-consuming, leading to neglect of other important aspects of your life such as family, work, and personal growth.

Benefits of Online Dating

That being said, online dating and social media can also be useful tools for connecting with like-minded individuals who share your faith and values.

Online dating allows you to broaden your pool of potential partners. In the past, we may have been limited to meeting people through our immediate social circle or at local events. However, with online dating, you can connect with individuals from all over the world who share your interests and values. This can lead to a more diverse and enriching dating experience, and can also increase your chances of finding a compatible partner.

Online dating allows you to be more intentional and selective in your search for a partner. You can use various filters and search criteria to narrow down your options and find individuals who align with your preferences and values. This can save time and energy compared to traditional dating methods, where you may have to go on multiple dates with people who are ultimately not a good match for you.

Social media can also be a powerful tool for discovering new communities and interests, building and maintaining relationships. It allows you to stay connected with friends and family members who live far away, and can facilitate communication and support in times of need.

Note of Caution

It's essential to approach these platforms with caution and set appropriate boundaries. Take the time to get to know someone before meeting in person, and be wary of strangers who are too eager to move things forward.

As Christians, your ultimate goal in dating should be to honour God and seek out relationships that are based on trust, mutual respect, and shared values. So, before diving headfirst into the world of online dating, pause and ask yourself, "What does God wants for me?" Pray and seek his guidance in your search for a partner. Trust in his plan for your life, knowing that he has your best interests at heart.

You should always strive to maintain your integrity and avoid behaviours that compromise your beliefs, even in the midst of the complex and ever-changing world of online dating and social media.

Exploring the Changing Dynamics of Gender Roles: A Biblical Perspective

As a generation, we are witnessing a shift in traditional gender roles and expectations. Historically, men were expected to take the lead in pursuing romantic relationships and providing for their families, while women were expected to prioritise their domestic duties and support their husbands. But in today's society, the traditional roles of the past are no longer the norm. Women are now pursuing careers outside of the home, and men are taking on more domestic responsibilities.

This has affected the dating technique as well, with many women taking on more assertive and active roles in pursuing romantic relationships. This shift can be both empowering and confusing, especially as we seek to understand what it means to reflect God's design for relationships and what works.

As Christians, it's important to approach these changing gender roles with a biblical perspective, seeking to honour God and reflect His design for relationships.

First off, let's get one thing straight. God created men and women differently, and that's a good thing. Men and women were designed to complement each other and work together to fulfil God's plan for humanity. The Bible says in Genesis 2:18, *"It is not good for the man to be alone. I will make a helper suitable for him."* Women were created to be helpers to men, and men were created to lead and provide for their families.

The Bible teaches in Genesis 1:27 that men and women are equal in value and worth yet, have different roles and responsibilities within the context of marriage. The Bible goes further to teach us that husbands should love their wives as Christ loved the church, and wives should submit to their husbands as the head of the household (Ephesians 5:22-33). Wives are expected to respect their husbands and submit to their leadership. These roles aren't based on cultural norms or societal expectations, but on God's design for marriage.

But here's the thing. These roles aren't meant to be restrictive or oppressive. Instead, they provide a framework for healthy and thriving relationships.

This is not about gender superiority or inferiority; it's about God's plan for marriage. It's about finding fulfilment and satisfaction within the role that God has given us. When husbands lead with love and selflessness, and wives submit with respect, both partners feel loved and valued and it creates a harmonious environment that honours God's design.

However, outside of marriage, there is more room for flexibility in gender roles and expectations. While men may still be expected to take the lead in initiating a relationship, women can and should feel empowered to communicate their own desires and expectations. It's important for both men and women to listen to each other's needs and communicate clearly and respectfully throughout the dating process.

But Christians should also be aware of cultural and societal pressures that may influence our expectations for gender roles in relationships. It's important to seek God's guidance in our relationships and to remember that while our roles and responsibilities may change, our fundamental identity as men and women created in God's image remains the same. Let's embrace each other's roles and work together to fulfil God's plan for our lives.

Beyond Casual Sex: The Risks of Hookup Culture for Christians

In our world today, it's clear that the concept of relationships has been turned upside down. You are bombarded with messages that tell you that casual sex is the norm and that hooking up with someone you barely know is the way to go. But as a Christian, you must remember that your values and beliefs are different from those of the world.

You must remember that sex is a gift from God, intended to be enjoyed within the confines of marriage (1 Corinthians 7:2-5). The Bible is clear about the consequences of sexual immorality (1 Corinthians 6:18), and you should take this warning seriously.

The so-called "hookup culture" is not only harmful to your physical health but also to your emotional and spiritual well-being. Physical risks can include sexually transmitted infections, unplanned pregnancy, and the emotional pain that often comes with casual sexual encounters. Emotional risks can include feelings of regret, shame, and low self-esteem. Spiritually, engaging in sex outside of marriage can lead you to feel disconnected from God and create a barrier to your relationship with Him.

The hookup culture also fosters a culture of objectification and dehumanization. When you engage in casual sex, you treat the other person as a means to an end, as an object to be used for your own pleasure. This can lead to a lack of respect for boundaries and consent, and can ultimately undermine the foundations of healthy and loving relationships. This goes against God's design for relationships, where we are called to love and respect one another (1 Peter 4:8).

It's important for you as a Christian to resist the pressures of the hookup culture and to seek out relationships that honour God and reflect His values. So, what can you do to resist the pressures of the hookup culture? First, you must remember your worth as a child of God and the value that He places on your body (1 Corinthians 6:19-20). You should set clear boundaries in your relationships and refuse to engage in casual sexual encounters. Ephesians 5:3 states, "*But among you there must not be even a hint of sexual immorality, or of any kind of impurity, or of greed, because these are improper for God's holy people.*"

But what if you've already made mistakes or feel trapped in the cycle of hookup culture? The good news is that we serve a God of grace and forgiveness. Through Christ's love and forgiveness, you can find healing and restoration, no matter what you've done in the past.

It's also important to extend grace and compassion to those who may have been hurt by the hookup culture or struggled with sexual sin. We should strive to create a culture of love and support, where individuals can find healing and restoration through the power of Christ's love and forgiveness. 1 John 1:9 reminds us, "*If we confess our sins, he is faithful and just and will forgive us our sins and purify us from all unrighteousness.*"

While the hookup culture may seem alluring and exciting, it ultimately leads to negative consequences and goes against God's design for relationships. Remember that the choices you make in your youth have a lasting impact on your life. It's important to choose wisely and with discernment, knowing that God has a plan for you and wants you to thrive in all aspects of your life, including your sexuality and relationships.

> **ACTION POINT:**
>
> *Write down your perspective about the new realities of dating boundaries and how they inform your perspectives going forward.*

Take home:

New waves require new skills to navigate safely.

Chapter 2

THE FOUNDATIONS OF CHRISTIAN DATING

What the Bible Says About Dating and Relationships

When it comes to love and relationships, everyone seems to have an opinion. But what does the Bible, the ultimate guidebook for life, says about it? It turns out, quite a lot! We know that God is love, and that love is at the core of our faith. In fact, the Bible tells us that "*God is love"* (1 John 4:8). So it's no surprise that the Bible has a lot to say about love and relationships. From the foundation of love to the importance of communication and putting God first, the Bible has all the wisdom and guidance we need to navigate the complex world of relationships.

It is essential to base your approach to dating on the principles laid out in the Bible. The Bible provides a solid foundation for dating that is grounded in God's love and wisdom.

One of the key teachings in the Bible about relationships is the importance of putting God first. In Matthew 22:37-38, Jesus says, *"Love the Lord your God with all your heart and with all your soul and with all your mind. This is the first and greatest commandment."* When you put God first in your life, you align yourself with His will and purpose for you. This helps you to make wise choices about who you date and how you conduct yourself in relationships.

Another crucial principle in the Bible about relationships is the importance of treating others with love and respect. In 1 Corinthians 13:4-7, one of the most famous passages in the Bible about love, Paul describes what true love looks like: *"Love is patient, love is kind. It does not envy, it does not boast, it is not proud. It does not dishonour others, it is not self-seeking, it is not easily angered, it keeps no record of wrongs. Love does not delight in evil but rejoices* with the truth. It always protects, always trusts, always hopes, always perseveres."

But what does this mean for your relationship? It means that true love is not just a feeling, but an action. These verses give you a clear picture of what healthy relationships should look like. You should treat each other with kindness, patience, and respect, avoiding behaviours such as envy, pride, and anger. You should always protect and trust your partner and be willing to work through difficulties with perseverance and always choosing to forgive.

Of course, it's also important to be careful about the company you keep. In 2 Corinthians 6:14, Paul warns against being unequally yoked with unbelievers: *"Do not be yoked together with unbelievers. For what do righteousness and wickedness have in common? Or what fellowship can light have with darkness?"* This does not mean that you cannot form friendships with non-Christians, but it does mean that you should be careful about entering into romantic relationships with people who do not share your faith.

So dear reader, as you navigate the world of dating and relationships, keep God at the centre of everything you do. By following these principles laid out in the Bible, you can build healthy and fulfilling relationships that honour God and bring you joy. Remember, God wants the very best for you, and He has given you everything you need to make wise choices in dating and relationships. With God's guidance, you can build the healthy and fulfilling relationships you've always dreamed of.

Understanding God's Plan for Marriage

God's plan for marriage is nothing short of a beautiful masterpiece, crafted with precision and purpose. The Bible teaches that marriage is not just a human institution, but a divine one - a sacred covenant between one man and one woman, designed to reflect the unending love and commitment that God has for us.

Marriage is a significant part of God's plan for humanity, and the Bible teaches us much about what a godly marriage should look like. In the book of Genesis, God created Adam and Eve and established the institution of marriage: *"Therefore a man shall leave his father and his mother and hold fast to his wife, and they shall become one flesh"* (Genesis 2:24).

God's plan for marriage is that it should be a lifelong commitment between one man and one woman, rooted in love and mutual respect and sustained by a deep and abiding faith in God. In Ephesians 5:25, husbands are called to love their wives as Christ loved the church, giving himself up for her. This means that husbands are called to sacrificially love and serve their wives, putting their needs before their own and guiding their families with wisdom and compassion.

Similarly, wives are called to submit to their husbands as to the Lord (Ephesians 5:22). This does not mean that wives should be subservient to their husbands or that husbands have the right to dominate their wives. Instead, it means that wives should respect and support their husbands in their role as leaders of the household.

At the heart of God's plan for marriage is sexual purity and faithfulness. In 1 Corinthians 6:18, Paul warns against sexual immorality, saying that it is a sin against one's own body. Hebrews 13:4 teaches that the *marriage bed should be kept pure and that marriage should be honoured by all.*

By understanding God's plan for marriage, you can approach dating and relationships with a clearer understanding of what you are looking for in a partner. You can search for a partner who share your values and is committed to building a God-honouring marriage. You can also strive to live your life in a way that honours God, whether you are single or in a relationship.

But the goal of dating and relationships is not just to find happiness, fulfilment or just about finding the right partner - it's also about seeking God's will for your life and to honour Him in all that you do. By following God's plan for marriage, you can build healthy and fulfilling relationships that bring glory to God and serve as a testimony to His love and faithfulness.

So pursue God's plan for marriage with all your heart, trusting in His wisdom and guidance as you seek to build relationships that honour Him. And remember that in God's hands, your relationships can become a beautiful masterpiece, reflecting His perfect love and grace to the world.

The Role of Prayer in Christian Dating

Imagine going on a hike in the wilderness without a map or a compass. You would likely end up lost, confused, and frustrated. In the same way, navigating the world of dating and relationships without prayer can leave you feeling lost and uncertain. But when you approach dating with prayer, you invite God to be a part of your journey, seeking His guidance and wisdom every step of the way. Prayer is an essential part of the Christian life, and it is just as crucial in the context of dating and relationships.

When you pray for guidance in your relationships, you tap into the wisdom of the One who created you and knows you better than you know yourself. In Proverbs 3:5-6, you are reminded to "*trust in the Lord with all your heart and lean not on your own understanding; in all your ways submit to him, and he will make your paths straight.*" One of the most significant benefits of praying in Christian dating is that it helps you to discern God's will for your life. When you pray for clarity and guidance in your relationship, you can trust that God will lead you in the right direction. In James 1:5, we are encouraged to ask God for wisdom: "*If any of you lacks wisdom, you should ask God, who gives generously to all without finding fault, and it will be given to you.*"

Think about it this way: when you're in a new relationship, it's like planting a seed. You can't just expect it to grow on its own; it needs care and attention to flourish. Prayer is the nourishment the seed needs to grow strong and healthy.

And just like how a plant needs sunlight to thrive, your relationship needs God's light and guidance to reach its full potential.

But prayer is not just about asking God for guidance; it's also about leaning on Him for strength and support when you face challenges in your relationships. Whether it's a disagreement with your partner or a struggle with temptation, you can turn to God in prayer, knowing that He will give you the wisdom and strength to overcome. In Philippians 4:6-7, we are reminded to *"not be anxious about anything, but in every situation, by prayer and petition, with thanksgiving, present your requests to God. And the peace of God, which transcends all understanding, will guard your hearts and your minds in Christ Jesus."*

When you turn to God in prayer, you acknowledge your weakness and your need for His strength. And in doing so, you open yourself up to experience the power of His love and grace in your relationship. In 2 Corinthians 12:9-10, Paul writes, "*But he said to me, 'My grace is sufficient for you, for my power is made perfect in weakness.' Therefore I will boast all the more gladly about my weaknesses, so that Christ's power may rest on me. That is why, for Christ's sake, I delight in weaknesses, in insults, in hardships, in persecutions, in difficulties. For when I am weak, then I am strong.*

Furthermore, prayer can help you to cultivate a deeper connection with God and with your partner. When you pray together as partners, you invite God to be a part of your relationship, strengthening your bond and deepening your love for each other. Ecclesiastes 4:12 says "*a cord of three strands is not quickly broken.*" When you make prayer a regular part of your relationship, you weave a strong cord between yourself, your partner and God, creating a bond that is difficult to break.

In Matthew 18:20, Jesus says, "*For where two or three gather in my name, there am I with them.*" When you pray together, you invite God into your relationship, and you can trust that He will bless your efforts to building a healthy and God-honouring relationship.

Prayer is the compass that guides you on your journey through the world of dating and relationships. By making prayer a priority in your dating life, you can trust that God will guide you in the right direction, give you the strength to overcome challenges, and help you to cultivate deeper connections with Him and with your partner. So if you're in an existing relationship or starting a new one, don't forget to make prayer a priority. Whether you're praying for wisdom and guidance, thanking God for your partner, or asking for His help in overcoming challenges, know that He is always listening and always ready to guide you toward the best possible outcome.

Role And Influence Of Parent In Dating Choices

We believe that parents have an important role to play in the lives of their children, including in matters of dating and relationships. Parents can offer guidance, support, and wisdom to their children as they navigate the complex world of dating. This may involve setting boundaries, discussing values and beliefs, and helping their children to make wise choices when it comes to relationships.

Parents can set expectations for their children when it comes to dating. This may include discussing the values and beliefs that guide their family, and making it clear what is and isn't acceptable behaviour in a dating relationship. By doing so, parents can help to ensure that their children are making wise choices and are protecting themselves from potential harm.

Parents should be actively involved in their children's dating lives. This means taking an interest in who their children are dating, asking questions, and offering guidance and support as needed. Rather than being overbearing, this involvement should demonstrate the parent's concern for their child and desire for them to make choices that are right.

Parents should pray for their children's dating lives. As Christians, we believe that prayer is powerful and can have a real impact on the lives of our children. By praying for their children's relationships, parents can offer spiritual support and guidance, and can trust that God will guide their children as they make choices about dating and relationships.

At the same time, it is important for young adults to take responsibility for their own choices and to seek God's guidance in their dating lives. While parental influence can be valuable, ultimately, it is up to each individual to discern what is right and to make choices that align with their faith and values.

ACTION POINT

Reflect on a time when God's plan for your life led you to unexpected places. How did this shape your perspective on dating?

Take home:

Be intentional in your dating relationships, keeping God's plan at the forefront.

Chapter 8

PREPARING FOR DATING

Self-Discovery: Building Self-Worth and Personal Growth

Before you enter the dating scene, it is essential that you take the time to reflect on yourself, your values, and your goals. This process of self-reflection is crucial for personal growth, and it can help you to develop a healthy sense of self-worth that is essential for successful dating.

Your sense of self-worth should be rooted in your identity in Christ. You are created in the image of God (Genesis 1:27), and you are valued and loved by Him. In Isaiah 43:4, God says, *"You are precious in my sight, and honoured, and I love you."* You should strive to see yourself as God sees you - valuable and worthy! You don't need to search for validation from others or settle for less than you deserve.

Self-reflection also involves taking an honest look at your strengths and weaknesses. By identifying areas where you need to grow and improve, you can take steps to become the best versions of yourself. Proverbs 27:17 says, "*Iron sharpens iron, and one man sharpens another.*"

By identifying areas for growth and seeking out mentors and friends who can help you along the way, you can become better equipped for successful relationships. Of course, personal growth doesn't just happen overnight. It requires intentional effort. This process of personal growth is essential for healthy relationships, as it helps you to develop the qualities and characteristics that are essential for successful dating.

In addition to self-reflection, personal growth also involves taking care of yourself in all areas including physically, emotionally, and spiritually. This means prioritizing self-care activities that nourish your body, mind, and soul. You can't pour into others if your own cup is empty. It also involves cultivating a deeper relationship with God, through studying the Bible, praying, and fellowshipping with other believers.

By prioritizing self-reflection, self-worth, and personal growth, we can approach dating with confidence, knowing that we are secured in our identity in Christ and that we have developed the qualities and characteristics that are essential for healthy relationships. We can also trust that God will lead us to partners who share our values and are committed to building a God-honouring relationship.

It's like preparing for a race: you need to train and get in shape before you can run it successfully. In the same way, you need to prepare yourself before entering into a relationship. Think about it: if you don't know who you are, what you want, and what you stand for, how can you expect to find a partner who aligns with those values? That's why it's so crucial to take the time to reflect on yourself and your goals before diving into the dating pool. As the saying goes, "know thyself."

As you prepare for dating, remember the words in Proverbs 4:23, which says, "*Above all else, guard your heart, for everything you do flows from it.*" By prioritizing your personal growth and relationship with God, you can guard your heart and approach dating with wisdom and discernment, seeking His will for your life and trusting in His guidance every step of the way.

Just like a gardener prepares the soil before planting the seeds, you must prepare yourself before jumping into the dating game. Now, get to work and prepare for God's best!

Identifying and Addressing Emotional Baggage

Imagine you're on a journey, and you're carrying a heavy backpack filled with all your past hurts, traumas, and negative experiences. As you walk, the weight becomes heavier and heavier, and it starts to slow you down, making it difficult for you to move forward. This backpack is your emotional baggage, and it can be a significant obstacle to healthy relationships and personal growth.

We all have emotional baggage of some sort. It could be the result of past relationships that have ended badly, childhood experiences that have left us with deep wounds, or even negative self-talk that we've internalized over time. Whatever the cause, it can affect our ability to trust, communicate, and connect with others.

So, what can you do about it? The first step is to take an honest assessment of your past experiences and recognize the ways in which they may be affecting your present attitudes and behaviours. Then, you may involve the guidance of a therapist or counsellor. They can provide a safe and supportive space to explore your emotions and work through past traumas and issues. You can also seek guidance and support from your church community by participating in prayer meetings, discipleship class, and church services.

You must be willing to examine the ways in which your past experiences may be affecting your present attitudes and behaviours, and work towards healing and growth.

But addressing your emotional baggage is not just about seeking external help. You must also practice self-compassion and forgiveness. You must learn to extend grace and forgiveness to yourself, recognizing that you are not defined by your past mistakes or experiences. Instead, you can choose to see yourself as God sees you, as a beloved child who is forgiven and redeemed through Christ.

Second Corinthians 5:17, reminds us that "if anyone is in Christ, the new creation has come: The old has gone, the new is here!" Through Christ, you can let go of your emotional baggage and embrace a new identity in Him. You can approach dating with a renewed sense of clarity and openness. You can develop healthier patterns of communication and behaviour, and build relationships based on trust and mutual respect. Most importantly, you can trust in God's love and guidance, knowing that He can heal your heart and lead you towards a healthy and fulfilling relationship.

In Matthew 11:28-29, Jesus invites you to come to Him with your burdens and find rest. He says, "Come to me, all you who are weary and burdened, and I will give you rest. Take my yoke upon you and learn from me, for I am gentle and humble in heart, and you will find rest for your souls." By entrusting your emotional baggage to Him, you can find healing and rest in His love, and approach dating with a renewed sense of hope and purpose.

So, dear reader, don't let your emotional baggage weigh you down. Take the necessary steps to address it, and trust in God's love and guidance. He will help you to move forward, build healthy relationships, and fulfil the purpose He has for your life.

Family and Culture: Balancing Expectations in Relationships

When it comes to dating and relationships, cultural and familial expectations can be like chains that weigh us down. Many young Christians face the challenge of finding the right balance between their faith and the cultural norms around them, and it's not always easy.

Examples of cultural and familial expectations might include pressure to marry within a certain community or social class, expectations around gender roles and responsibilities within a relationship, or cultural taboos around certain behaviours or activities. These expectations can hinder your freedom to choose whom you love and how you express it.

But fear not, for God's Word provides guidance on how you can break free from cultural shackles and pursue relationships that are true to your faith. It starts with prayerfully considering your own values and beliefs, and seeking God's guidance in your dating relationships. This may involve having difficult conversations with family members or cultural communities, and setting boundaries around certain expectations or behaviours that conflict with your faith.

As you navigate these expectations, it's important to remember that your dating partner may also come from a different cultural background. In 1 Corinthians 9:22, Paul says to *become all things to all people, so that we may win them over to Christ*. This means respecting and appreciating your partner's culture, while also staying true to your own beliefs and values. It is therefore important to communicate openly and honestly with your dating partner, and seek to understand their own cultural and familial expectations.

At the end of the day, your ultimate goal is to honour God in your dating relationship, and seek to glorify Him in all that you do. This may mean setting aside cultural or familial expectations that conflict with your faith, and prioritising your relationship with God above all else.

Romans 12:2, says we are not to conform to the patterns of this world, but to be transformed by the renewing of our minds.

Consider the story of Ruth in the Bible. Ruth was a Moabite woman who married into an Israelite family. Despite her family belief system and culture, she chose to acknowledge the One and only True God. She didn't follow her family's patterns of idol worshipping. When her husband and father-in-law died, she chose to remain with her mother-in-law, Naomi, and followed her to Israel. Ruth's story is a powerful example of someone who chose to honour God above all else, even in the face of cultural and societal expectations. By remaining faithful to Naomi and choosing to follow God's plan, Ruth was ultimately blessed with a loving relationship and a place in God's family.

Like Ruth, you too can trust in God's guidance and wisdom as you navigate cultural and familial expectations in your dating relationship. By seeking His will above all else, you can build relationships that honour Him and bring joy and fulfilment to your life.

> **ACTION POINT**
>
> *Evaluate your current relationship. Are there any areas where you need to set stronger boundaries or improve overall?*

Take home:

Prioritize your relationship with God above all else.

Chapter 4

BUILDING HEALTHY RELATIONSHIPS

Balancing Individual Needs and Relationship Goals in Christian Dating

In any Christian relationship, it is important to strike a balance between individual needs and relationship goals. While it is important to maintain a sense of individuality and pursue personal growth and interests, it is equally important to prioritize the relationship and work towards shared goals.

Let's picture a couple who are deeply in love, but each has their own unique goals and desires. One partner dreams of traveling the world and exploring new cultures, while the other has a passion for starting their own business. Balancing these individual needs and desires with their shared goals as a couple can be challenging, but it is crucial for the success of their relationship. As they navigate these conflicting goals, they must communicate openly and honestly, and be willing to make compromises and sacrifices for each other. This might mean delaying their travel plans or starting a business together that aligns with both of their passions and goals.

Balancing individual needs and relationship goals can often be a delicate dance, as it requires open communication, compromise, and a willingness to put the needs of the relationship before individual desires. For example, if one partner is pursuing a demanding career or education path, it may be necessary for the other partner to make sacrifices in order to support their goals and maintain a healthy relationship.

At the same time, it is important for both partners to maintain a sense of individuality and pursue their own interests and passions. This can help to maintain a sense of excitement and novelty in the relationship, and prevent either partner from feeling stifled or unfulfilled.

Ultimately, balancing individual needs and relationship goals requires a willingness to communicate openly and honestly, to make compromises and sacrifices when necessary, and to support and encourage each other as individuals and as a couple. As Philippians 2:4 reminds us, *"Let each of you look not only to his own interests, but also to the interests of others."* By prioritizing both individual needs and relationship goals, a Christian couple can build a strong and healthy relationship that will last a lifetime.

So, find your balance. Pursue your passions, but don't forget to prioritize your partner and work together towards shared goals.

The Role of Compatibility in a Successful Christian Relationship

In a world where you have so many options and choices available to you, finding someone who is compatible with you is important in building a successful Christian relationship. But what does compatibility really mean? And how do you know if you are truly compatible with your partner?

Compatibility refers to the ability of two people to live and work together in a harmonious and complementary way. In a Christian relationship, this means sharing common values, beliefs, and goals, as well as being able to communicate and understand each other's needs and desires. It's like two puzzle pieces that fit perfectly together, creating a beautiful and complete picture.

While having differences can sometimes add excitement and novelty to a relationship, a lack of compatibility can often lead to conflicts and misunderstandings.

One way to identify compatibility is to evaluate your level of similarity in key areas such as faith, interests, and values. Are you both equally committed to your Christian faith? Do you have similar beliefs about important moral issues? Additionally, sharing similar life goals, such as a desire to start a family, finance or pursue a certain career, can help to ensure that the relationship is moving in the same direction.

By considering these factors, you can check and know if you have a strong foundation for building a successful Christian relationship.

Another important aspect of compatibility is emotional compatibility. This refers to the ability of two people to connect emotionally and feel comfortable and supported in each other's presence. This involves being able to communicate effectively, understand each other's needs and feelings, and be responsive to each other's emotional states.

Compatibility is so important in Christian dating as it can prevent a lot of conflicts and misunderstandings. Imagine being in a relationship where you have completely different beliefs and morals, or where you have different life goals. It can be exhausting to constantly try to navigate these differences, and it can often lead to disagreements that could have been avoided if you were more compatible.

However, it is important to note that compatibility does not mean that two people have to be identical or share every interest or hobby. It is possible to have differences and still be compatible as long as both parties are willing to communicate and respect each other's differences, to compromise and find common ground.

Compatibility can play a key role in building a successful Christian relationship. When two people share similar values, interests, and lifestyles, they can build a strong bond that will help them weather any storm. Remember, a successful relationship is not just about finding the perfect partner, but also about being the right partner. As Colossians 3:14 says, *"Above all, love each other deeply, because love covers over a multitude of sins."*

The Power of Communication in Christian Dating

You must understand the importance of communication in every aspect of your life. The Bible teaches us that communication is vital to our relationships with God and with others. In the book of Proverbs, we read that *"A word fitly spoken is like apples of gold in pictures of silver"* (Proverbs 25:11, KJV). This passage tells us that the way you communicate has the power to bring beauty and value to your relationships.

Communication is the key to unlocking the full potential of your relationship! I'm talking about open and honest communication. You see, when you communicate with your partner, you're not just talking about the weather or your favourite TV show. You're opening up about your hopes, dreams, and fears. You're letting them see the real you, and in turn, you're learning more about them too. By communicating effectively and honestly with your dating partners, you can build trust, establish shared values and goals, and deepen your emotional connection.

One important aspect of communication is being clear about your intentions and expectations. This involves having open and honest conversations about your faith, your values, and your vision for the future. By being transparent about your desires and goals, you can avoid misunderstandings and build a strong foundation for your relationship.

Communication is not just about talking, but also about active listening. This involves truly hearing and understanding your dating partner's perspective, and seeking to empathise with their experiences and feelings. By actively listening, you demonstrate respect and care for your partner. It shows that you care and value their perspective and build deeper levels of trust and intimacy. You can do this by asking questions, repeating what you've heard, and showing empathy and having understanding.

Likewise, it is important to communicate respectfully and kindly, even in moments of conflict. This may involve using "I" statements to express your own feelings and perspectives, rather than blaming or attacking your partner. Ephesians 4:15 tells us to "*speak the truth in love,*" which means that you need to be honest with your partner, but you also need to communicate with kindness and compassion. You need to be mindful of your words and actions, and you need to seek God's guidance in your communication. By approaching conflicts with kindness and empathy, you can avoid damaging your relationship and instead use them as an opportunity for growth and learning.

Communication is a powerful tool that can make or break your relationship. As Proverbs 18:21 reminds us, "*Death and life are in the power of the tongue, and those who love it will eat its fruits.*" So don't be afraid to speak up, listen closely, and use the power of your words to build a beautiful and fulfilling relationship.

Understanding Consent and Boundaries in Christian Dating

Your body and emotions are sacred and you must protect them. That's why you must set clear limits for yourself and communicate them to your partner. You may think that consent and boundaries only apply to physical intimacy, but they extend to every aspect of our relationship.

These limits may include boundaries around physical intimacy, emotional vulnerability, or even things like time and money. By doing so, you can create a safe and secure environment that fosters mutual respect and trust.

In Christian dating, it is important to understand the concepts of consent and boundaries. Consent involves obtaining clear and enthusiastic agreement from your dating partner before engaging in any physical or emotional activity. This can involve checking in with your partner and respecting their wishes at every stage of the relationship.

Boundaries, on the other hand, are the limits you set for yourself and communicate to your dating partner. These include areas of your life that you want to protect or safeguard. By respecting your own boundaries and those of your partner, you can build a relationship that is healthy, respectful, and fulfilling.

Consent and boundaries should be discussed openly and honestly with your dating partner. This may involve having conversations about your desires and limits, and being willing to hear and respect your partner's wishes as well.

You should also be willing to respect your partner's decision if they choose to set a boundary that you may not agree with. It's essential to understand that everyone has their limits, and it's not your place to pressure or coerce your partner into doing something they're not comfortable with. By respecting their boundaries, you show that you value and care for them, which can deepen your emotional connection and strengthen your relationship.

By prioritising our partner's wishes and respecting our own boundaries, we can build a relationship that is based on respect, trust and mutual love. As Christians, we are called to love and honour one another, and that includes respecting each other's boundaries and desires. As 1 Corinthians 10:23

reminds us, *"All things are lawful,"* but not all things are helpful. *"All things are lawful,"* but not all things build up.

Red Flags and Warning Signs in Christian Relationships

While Christian dating can be a fulfilling and joyful experience, it is important to recognize red flags and warning signals that may indicate an unhealthy or even abusive relationship. These may include:

1. **Lack of Respect:** If your dating partner consistently belittles or undermines you, or shows disrespect towards your values or beliefs, this may be a red flag. For example, if they dismiss your opinions or mock your faith, this may indicate that they do not value you as a person.

2. **Control:** If your dating partner tries to control or manipulate you, this may be a warning sign. For example, if they insist on making all the decisions or try to isolate you from your friends and family, this may indicate that they are seeking to exert power and control over you. If your dating partner

tries to control who you spend time with, what you wear, or what you do, this may be a warning sign of an unhealthy relationship. Both partners should have the freedom to make their own choices and pursue their own interests.

3. **Manipulation:** If your dating partner uses guilt, threats, or other manipulative tactics to get their way, this may be a warning sign of an unhealthy relationship. Healthy relationships are based on mutual trust and respect, not coercion or manipulation.

4. **Jealousy and Possessiveness:** If your dating partner is excessively jealous or possessive, this may be a red flag. For example, if they become angry or upset when you spend time with friends or pursue your own interests, this may indicate that they do not trust you or have a healthy sense of boundaries.

5. **Verbal or Emotional Abuse:** If your dating partner engages in verbal, emotional or physical abuse, this is a clear warning sign. This may include name-calling, put-downs, threats, or other forms of abusive behaviour.

6. **Physical abuse:** Any form of physical violence, including hitting, pushing, or shoving, is a major warning sign of an abusive relationship. If you or someone you know is facing physical abuse, it is important to seek help immediately.

7. **Dishonesty and Deceit:** If your dating partner is consistently dishonest or deceitful, this may be a red flag. For example, if they lie about their past, their intentions, or their actions, this may indicate that they are not trustworthy or may be hiding something from you.

These are just a few examples of warning signals and red flags that may indicate an unhealthy or even abusive relationship. It is also noteworthy that red flags and warning signs may not always be obvious, and that abusive behaviour can be disguised as love or concern. If you notice any of these behaviours in your dating partner, it is important to take them seriously and consider whether this is a relationship that is truly healthy and fulfilling for you. 1

Corinthians 15:33 says, *"Do not be deceived: 'Bad company ruins good morals.'"*

Conflict Resolution and Forgiveness in Christian Relationships

Listen up, no relationship is perfect. Conflicts are inevitable in any relationship, including Christian ones. However, the way conflicts are handled can make all the difference in the health and durability of a relationship. Conflict resolution and forgiveness are critical components of a successful Christian relationship.

Conflict resolution involves actively working towards resolving any issues that may arise in a relationship. This can involve having open and honest communication, active listening, and a willingness to compromise. And to add on, it takes humility to approach conflict resolution the right way. You need to have a heart that desires to maintain the relationship.

Forgiveness is also an important aspect of a Christian relationship. Forgiveness involves choosing to let go of past hurts and allowing the relationship to move forward. It is important to remember that forgiveness is not the same as forgetting or condoning harmful behaviour. Instead, it involves choosing to release any resentment or bitterness towards the other person. This can be a difficult and painful process, but it is necessary for the healing of your hearts and your relationships.

In Matthew 18:21-22, Peter asked Jesus how many times he should forgive someone who has sinned against him, and Jesus responded, "*Not seven times, but seventy times seven.*" This shows the importance of forgiveness in Christian relationships and means that forgiveness is not just a one-time act but a continuous choice that you must make every day.

Conflict resolution and forgiveness are crucial components of a successful Christian relationship. By approaching conflicts with humility, open communication, and a willingness to compromise, and by choosing to forgive past hurts, couples can work towards building a strong and healthy relationship that honours God. Colossians 3:13 tells us to *forgive as the Lord forgave us*. Strive to forgive others as you have been forgiven and allow the love and grace of God to heal your hearts and your relationships.

> **ACTION POINT**
>
> *Think about a red flag you ignored in a past relationship. How can you use this experience to make better decisions in the future?*

Take home:

Look for compatibility in a potential partner rather than solely physical attraction.

Chapter 5

NAVIGATING BREAKUPS AND REJECTION

How to handle rejection and breakups in a healthy way

Breaking up can be one of the most excruciating experiences, especially when it happens in a Christian relationship. But in the midst of the pain and heartbreak, it's important to remember that there is hope for healing and growth. As Psalm 147:3 reminds us, *"He heals the broken-hearted and binds up their wounds."* So if you're facing rejection or a breakup, know that you are not alone and that God is with you every step of the way.

With the right mindset and support, you can navigate this tumultuous terrain with grace and resilience. So, how do you handle rejection and breakups in a healthy way?

Focus on self-care

One of the most important things to remember when facing rejection or a breakup is to take care of yourself emotionally and spiritually. Imagine yourself as a beautiful flower that needs nurturing and care to bloom. By taking care of yourself and approaching the situation with empathy and understanding, and finding your worth in God, you can navigate rejection and breakups in a healthy and empowering way. Proverbs 17:22 says *"A cheerful heart is good medicine, but a crushed spirit dries up the bones."* By focusing on self-care, you can help lift your spirits and find hope in the midst of heartbreak.

Seek God's Wisdom and Direction

Pray for guidance and wisdom on how to move forward. Ask God to show you what He wants you to learn from the experience and how He wants you to use it for His glory.

Don't play the blame game

Resist the temptation to blame yourself or your ex-partner for the breakup. Instead, try to approach the situation with empathy and understanding, and focus on finding ways to grow and learn from the experience. Remember that God has a plan for your life, and that everything happens for a reason.

It is important to remember that rejection and breakups do not define your worth or value as a person. You are a beloved child of God, and your worth and identity come from Him alone. 1 Peter 5:7, *"Cast all your anxiety on him because he cares for you."*

Allow Yourself to Grieve

One of the most important things to do after experiencing heartbreak is to allow yourself to grieve. It's okay to feel sad, angry, or confused. Give yourself time to process your emotions and don't rush the healing process. Ecclesiastes 3:4 says there is *"a time to weep and a time to laugh, a time to mourn and a time to dance."* Take comfort in the fact that God is with you in your grief.

Practice Forgiveness

Forgiveness is key to finding healing and moving forward. Forgive your ex-partner and yourself for any hurtful actions or mistakes made during the relationship. Remember that forgiveness is not ignoring or justifying the behaviour but releasing the hold it has on your life.

Find Support from Your Community

One of the most important sources of hope and healing after heartbreak is the support of your community. This can include friends, family, a support group, or a professional counsellor. Don't be afraid to reach out for help and support during this time. Galatians 6:2 says, *"Bear one another's burdens, and so fulfil the law of Christ."* Your community can help carry you through this difficult time.

Don't make hasty decisions

Another important aspect of handling rejection and breakups in a healthy way is to avoid making hasty or impulsive decisions that you may regret later. This may include avoiding the temptation to seek revenge or to jump into a new relationship too quickly.

Instead, take time to reflect on your feelings and needs, and focus on rebuilding your sense of self-worth and confidence. This may involve engaging in activities that bring you joy and fulfilment, such as hobbies or volunteering, and seeking out new experiences and opportunities for personal growth.

Don't rush it

Remember that the healing process takes time, and that it is important to be patient and compassionate with yourself during this journey. With the right mindset and support, you can emerge from a breakup or rejection stronger and more resilient than ever before.

While breakups and rejection can be painful, they can also offer chances for growth and self-discovery. Heartbreak is a painful and difficult experience, but it is not the end of your story.

Finding hope and healing after heartbreak

Heartbreak can be a difficult and emotional process for anyone, especially for young people who are still discovering their way in life. It can be hard to find hope and healing after a breakup or a rejection. However, with the support of loved ones and a strong faith, it is possible to find hope and healing in the aftermath of heartbreak.

Stay Positive

Instead of dwelling on negative emotions or past mistakes, try to focus on the good things in your life and the blessings you have. This may involve practicing gratitude through journaling or daily affirmations, and seeking out positive and uplifting experiences.

Seek God's Guidance and Comfort

True healing and hope come from God. Psalm 147:3 says, "He heals the broken-hearted and binds up their wounds." Spend time studying God's Word, praying and asking God for guidance and comfort during this difficult time. Remember that God is always with you, and He can provide the peace and strength you need to move forward.

Lean on your faith during this time, and trust in God's plan for your life. As Romans 8:28 reminds us that all things work together for good to those who love God.

Seek for professional help

Getting professional support such as therapy or counselling can be very helpful. A qualified therapist can offer support and guidance as you navigate the healing process, and can help you to identify and address any underlying issues or patterns that may be contributing to your heartbreak.

Sometimes, heartbreak can feel like the end of the world, but it's important to remember that it's only for a season. Even though it may feel like the pain will never end, there is hope for healing and restoration. The Bible tells us in Isaiah 43:18-19, *"Forget the former things; do not dwell on the past. See, I am doing a new thing! Now it springs up; do you not perceive it? I am making a way in the wilderness and streams in the wasteland."* God has a plan for your life, and He is faithful to bring beauty from ashes.

Remember that healing is a journey. And so as you take care of yourself emotionally and spiritually, getting the needed support and guidance, you can find hope and healing after heartbreak.

> ***ACTION POINT***
>
> *Practice forgiveness and extend grace to those who have hurt you in the past.*

Take home:

Healing and hope are possible after heartbreak.

Chapter 6

PERSONALIZED STORIES ABOUT DATING

Real-life dating experiences shared by Christian parents and young adults

In this chapter, we will be sharing real-life dating experiences from Christian parents and young adults (*Not their real names*). These stories provide insight and inspiration for navigating the complex world of dating today, and highlight the importance of staying true to your values and faith.

A Journey to Finding Love Through Faith

When Julia's daughter, Enny, struggled to find a partner who shared her Christian values, she couldn't help but worry. Enny had faced disappointment and heartbreak in several relationships, but she refused to compromise on her beliefs. One day, after a particularly tough breakup, Enny decided to take a bold step and put her love life on hold.

As she invested time in deepening her relationship with God, Enny found a sense of peace and contentment in her singleness that she had never experienced before. Through her journey of prayer and self-reflection, she learned to trust in God's plan for her life and let go of her fears and doubts.

It wasn't until Enny met Seyi through a mutual friend at church that things began to change. As they got to know each other better, Enny realized that this man shared her faith and values, and they eventually began dating.

With God at the centre of their relationship, Enny and Seyi were able to build a strong foundation of love and trust.

Finding Love Online: A Christian's Journey

Meet Ola, a devout Christian who was looking for love. He had tried traditional methods of meeting people, but nothing seemed to work. One day, he decided to give online dating a try. At first, he was apprehensive about the idea, but he was willing to take a chance.

Ola knew that finding a partner who shared his faith and values was important to him, so he made sure to be upfront about his beliefs in his dating profile. This way, he could weed out anyone who wasn't serious about their faith.

After some time, Ola met Jenny. They hit it off immediately and spent weeks talking online before they decided to meet in person. Jenny was also a Christian and shared similar values with Ola. They went on their first date and immediately hit it off. They enjoyed each other's company, and their conversation flowed effortlessly. Ola felt a strong connection with Jenny and was hopeful that this could be something special.

As they continued to date, Ola and Jenny took their time getting to know each other. They spent time praying together, discussing their faith, and exploring each other's interests. Their relationship grew stronger each day.

Through the challenges of online dating, Ola learned that being upfront about his faith was crucial. By being open and honest, he was able to attract a partner who shared his values and beliefs. In the end, his journey led him to the love of his life.

Choosing Faith Over Love

Meet David, a young Christian man who dated a non-Christian woman for several months. Despite his concerns about their differing beliefs, he felt a strong connection with her and didn't want to end the relationship. He believed that their love for each other was strong enough to overcome any differences.

However, David's parents were worried about their son's relationship. They feared that his girlfriend's lack of faith will pull him away from his Christian beliefs. They tried to talk to him about their concerns, but David was convinced that everything will work out in the end.

As time went on, David began to have a conflict between his love for his girlfriend and his devotion to God. He realized that his faith is a fundamental part of his life and he needed a partner who shared those beliefs.

Feeling confused and torn, David decided to seek guidance from his pastor and spent time in prayer. Through his conversations with his pastor and his own introspection, he realized that he couldn't compromise his faith for the sake of his relationship.

With a heavy heart, David ended the relationship. Although it was painful at first, he found peace knowing that he is following God's plan for his life. He trusts that God will bring the right person into his life, someone who shares his faith and values.

A few months later, David attended a Christian conference and met a woman who shares his faith and values. They bond over their mutual love for God and their desire to build a relationship that honours Him. They started dating and got married.

David looks back on his previous relationship and realizes that he made the right decision by following God's plan. He is grateful for the love and support of his family and friends, and most of all, for the guidance of God in his life.

From Heartbreak to Happily Ever After

John had been through a series of heartbreaks and disappointing relationships. He started to believe that maybe finding someone who shared his faith and values was impossible. He felt discouraged and lonely.

One day, while scrolling through his phone, he stumbled upon a Christian dating app. At first, he was hesitant about online dating, but he decided to give it a try. After all, what did he have to lose?

It wasn't until he met Sarah that he knew he had made the right decision. They talked for hours on the app, sharing stories about their lives and faith. John was amazed at how easy it was to talk to Sarah, and he felt a strong connection with her right from the start.

As they continued to talk, John discovered that Sarah was the woman he had been waiting for. She shared his values and beliefs, and she was committed to living a life that glorified God. Their shared faith became the foundation of their relationship, and they felt blessed to have found each other.

Together, John and Sarah have experienced the beauty and joy of a loving relationship built on a strong foundation of faith. They know that their journey wasn't easy, but they also know that God's plan for their lives was worth waiting for.

These stories demonstrate the importance of staying true to your values and faith in the dating process, and highlight the power of prayer and reflection in finding the right partner. By sharing these experiences, I hope to inspire and encourage you on your own journey towards finding love and building healthy relationships.

Lessons learned from these experiences

From these stories, we can learn several important lessons about Christian dating:

1. *Stay true to your faith and values:* It can be tempting to compromise on your beliefs or values in order to make a relationship work, but ultimately this will only lead to frustration and disappointment. By staying true to your faith and values, you can find a partner who shares those same beliefs and build a strong, lasting relationship.

2. *Seek guidance and support:* When faced with difficult decisions or challenges in dating, it's important to seek guidance and support from trusted sources, such as a pastor or close friend. Prayer is also a powerful tool in discerning God's will for your life.

3. *Trust in God's plan:* Even when it feels like you're facing rejection or setbacks in your dating life, you can trust that God has a plan for you and that everything happens for a reason. By surrendering your desires and hopes to God, you can find peace and hope in knowing that His plan is perfect.

4. *Be open to new possibilities*: Sometimes, love can come from unexpected places, like a dating app or a Christian conference. It's important to keep an open mind and heart, and trust that God can bring love into your life in unexpected ways.

By applying these lessons to your own dating journey, you can approach the process with confidence, faith, and a spirit of openness and trust.

Locating God's word for difficult situation

When it comes to dating, there are several Bible verses that can provide guidance and comfort during difficult situations. Here are a few examples:

Proverbs 3:5-6: "Trust in the Lord with all your heart and lean not on your own understanding; in all your ways submit to him, and he will make your paths straight." This verse encourages you to trust in God's plan for your life, even when things don't go according to your own plans.

1 Corinthians 13:4-7: "Love is patient, love is kind. It does not envy, it does not boast, it is not proud. It does not dishonour others, it is not self-seeking, it is not easily angered, it keeps no record of wrongs. Love does not delight in evil but rejoices with the truth. It always protects, always trusts, always hopes, always perseveres." This verse reminds you of what true love looks like and encourages you to strive for it in your relationship.

Philippians 4:6-7: "Do not be anxious about anything, but in every situation, by prayer and petition, with thanksgiving, present your requests to God. And the peace of God, which transcends all understanding, will guard your hearts and your minds in Christ Jesus." This verse reminds you to involve God in all that you do especially in situations that are beyond your control. He is able solve the situation with a peace that surpasses all understanding, guarding your heart and mind in Christ Jesus. This can be particularly helpful in dating when you are unsure of the future or not certain about the direction of the relationship.

2 Corinthians 6:14: "Do not be yoked together with unbelievers. For what do righteousness and wickedness have in common? Or what fellowship can light have with darkness?" This verse warns against being in a relationship with someone who does not share your faith and values, as it can lead to conflicts and compromises.

Ecclesiastes 4:9-12: "Two are better than one, because they have a good return for their labour: If either of them falls down, one can help the other up. But pity anyone who falls and has no one to help them up. Also, if two lie down together, they will keep warm. But how can one keep warm alone? Though one may be overpowered, two can defend themselves. A cord of three strands is not quickly broken." This verse highlights the importance of having a supportive and loving partner in your life.

Romans 12:9: *"Let love be genuine. Abhor what is evil; hold fast to what is good."* This verse encourages you to approach love with sincerity and a commitment to doing what is right in God's eyes. It reminds you to prioritize moral purity and to steer clear of anything that goes against God's standards for your life.

> *Psalm 37:4: "Delight yourself in the Lord, and he will give you the desires of your heart."*

This verse reminds you that when you prioritize your relationship with God, he will give you the things that are best for you, including your relationship. By seeking first God's kingdom and righteousness, you can trust that he will provide you with a partner who aligns with his will for your life.

Psalm 34:18: "The Lord is close to the brokenhearted and saves those who are crushed in spirit," Romans 8:28: "And we know that in all things God works for the good of those who love him, who have been called according to his purpose." These verses remind you that God is near to you in your pain and sorrow, and He is willing to comfort and heal your broken hearts. It is a source of hope and strength to know that you are not alone in your struggles and that God is with you, guiding you through difficult times.

By turning to God's word for guidance, comfort, and wisdom, you'll be able to navigate the ups and downs of dating with faith and resilience.

> **ACTION POINT**
>
> *Share your dating experiences with a friend or mentor.*

> **Take home:**
>
> *Personal stories can be a powerful tool for learning.*

Chapter 7

MAINTAINING PURITY AND INTIMACY IN CHRISTIAN DATING

Overcoming societal pressure to be in a relationship

Have you ever felt like you're the odd one out because you're not in a relationship? Do you feel like society is constantly pressuring you to find love, even if it's not what you want or need right now? Today, there is a great deal of pressure to be in a relationship. Everywhere you look, from social media to advertising, you are bombarded with images of couples who are happy and in love. This can make it difficult for single individuals to resist the urge to pursue a relationship even if it is not in their best interest or align with their values.

It is important to remember that as a Christian, your worth is not defined by your relationship status. You are a unique individual created in the image of God, and your value comes from Him. You don't need a significant other to feel complete or fulfilled. You can trust in His timing and plan for your life, rather than giving into societal pressures.

The Bible says that you are never truly alone. Psalm 68:6 says, "*God sets the lonely in families.*" You can find support in your church and other Christian groups, even if you don't have a significant other. You can build important relationships with others and with God, which will bring you more joy and fulfilment than any romantic relationship ever could.

Surrounding yourself with supportive friends and family members who share your values and beliefs is a very good way to resist societal pressure. They can help you stay accountable and remind you of your worth in Christ and the importance of staying true to yourself and God's plan.

As well as focusing on personal growth and development to help you feel more content and fulfilled in your singleness. You can use this time to pursue your passions, develop new skills, and deepen your relationship with God.

So trust in God's plan for you, and know that He has great things in store for your future, whether or not that includes a romantic relationship right now.

Understanding God's Plan for Sexual Purity

Maintaining purity and intimacy in Christian dating may not be easy, but it is essential if you want to honour God with your body and your relationships. You see, sex was designed by God to be a beautiful expression of love between a husband and wife. It's a sacred and intimate act that should be reserved for marriage.

Therefore, as a Christian, you are called to honour God's plan for sexual purity and abstain from sexual immorality. The Bible is clear in its teachings on sexual purity. In 1 Corinthians 6:18-20, it states: *"Flee from sexual immorality. Every other sin a person commits is outside the body, but the sexually immoral person sins against his own body. Or do you not know that your body is a temple of the Holy Spirit within you, whom you have from God? You are not your own, for you were bought with a price. So glorify God in your body."*

This can be challenging in today's society, where sexual promiscuity is often encouraged and even celebrated. That's why it's so important to surround yourself with like-minded people who share your commitment to sexual purity. Seek out friends and mentors who will support you and hold you accountable, and avoid people and situations that could lead you astray.

Also, by relying on God's strength and guidance, you can maintain your commitment to sexual purity and avoid the harmful consequences of sexual immorality.

In addition to refraining from sexual activity outside of marriage, you must also guard your heart and mind in the area of sexual purity. This means avoiding pornographic material, inappropriate conversations, and anything else that could lead you down a path of sexual temptation.

Purity is more than just abstaining from sexual activity. It's about building healthy emotional connections with your partner, cultivating deep and meaningful relationships built on mutual respect and love. It's about honouring God with every aspect of your life, including your dating relationships.

So, if you're struggling with sexual purity, know that you're not alone. But also know that with God's help, you can overcome any temptation and stay pure. Pray for strength and guidance, and surround yourself with other believers who can support and encourage you in your journey.

Know this that, God's plan for sexual purity is not about limiting your pleasure - it's about protecting your heart, mind, and soul. It's about experiencing the fullness of God's love and grace in your relationships. Following God's plan for sexual purity is not always easy, but it is always worth it.

Mastering Physical Desires and Setting Healthy Boundaries in Dating

It's easy to feel overwhelmed by physical desires and societal pressure. Everywhere you turn, you're bombarded with messages about instant gratification and sexual liberation. However, it is important to remember that sexual intimacy is a gift and it is from God intended to be shared within the context of marriage.

Physical boundaries can differ from person to person, and it is crucial to establish them together as a couple, with respect for each other's individual comfort levels and values.

So, how can you navigate your physical desires and set healthy boundaries in your dating relationship?

1. ***Acknowledge and address your desires:*** It's important to acknowledge that physical desires are a natural part of being human, and there is nothing wrong with experiencing them. However, it's also essential to recognize that acting on these desires outside of marriage is not in line with Christian values. Couples should discuss their physical desires openly and honestly, and come up with strategies to address them in a healthy and godly way.

2. ***Establish clear boundaries:*** Setting boundaries is crucial in any relationship, but

it is especially important when it comes to physical intimacy. Couples should have a clear understanding of what is and isn't appropriate in their relationship. This could include guidelines for things like holding hands, kissing, or physical touch. It's important to establish these boundaries together, and to hold each other accountable to them.

3. ***Communicate openly and respectfully:*** Communication is key in any relationship, but it's especially important when it comes to physical desires and boundaries. Couples should talk openly and respectfully about their feelings and desires, and they also should be willing to listen to each other's concerns. It's important to remember that communication is a two-way street, and both partners should feel comfortable expressing their thoughts and feelings without fear of judgment.

4. ***Lean on God:*** Above all, overcoming physical desires and setting boundaries in a Christian relationship requires relying on

God's strength and wisdom. Couples should spend time praying and studying the bible together, and seeking God's guidance and direction for their relationship. They should also be willing to ask for help from trusted Christian mentors or counsellors when needed.

5. *Avoid tempting situations:* It's important to be aware of situations that may lead to temptation and to avoid them whenever possible. For example, if a couple finds that they struggle with physical temptation when they are alone in a private setting, they may choose to spend more time in public places or with friends.

6. *Have accountability measures:* This can involve confiding in trusted friends, family members, trusted Christian counsellors or mentors who can help hold you accountable to your boundaries and offer support and guidance when needed. Additionally, participating in support groups or seminars focused on relationships and sexuality can

provide a safe and supportive community for couples to discuss and navigate these issues.

Let's consider the story of Joseph and Potiphar's wife. In Genesis 39, we see how Joseph resists the advances of Potiphar's wife, even though she tries to seduce him repeatedly. Joseph's response is a powerful example of setting boundaries and prioritising God's plan for purity. He recognises that sexual intimacy is a gift from God to be shared within the context of marriage and refuses to compromise his values, even when it means facing persecution and imprisonment.

Like Joseph, you too can rely on God's strength and guidance to resist temptation and set healthy boundaries in your relationships. By prioritising purity and intimacy in your dating lives, you can honour God's plan and experience the true joy and fulfilment that comes from a deep and meaningful relationship built on mutual respect and love.

Ultimately, prioritising God's plan for purity and intimacy in Christian dating can help to foster a deeper connection with Him and with a potential future spouse.

The benefits of accountability and community

In Christian dating, accountability and community are crucial for maintaining purity and intimacy. It is important to have a support system of trusted friends and mentors who can provide guidance and encouragement in difficult situations.

Accountability partners can hold each other accountable for sticking to agreed-upon boundaries and can provide a listening ear and prayer support. They can also help identify potential red flags or warning signs in a relationship.

Community can provide a sense of belonging and fellowship, and can also offer opportunities for healthy social interactions and alternative activities to avoid temptation. Church groups, Bible studies, and other Christian organisations can be wonderful avenues to meet like-minded people who share similar values and beliefs. The wisdom gained from older mentors and peers can be priceless in navigating the complications of dating and relationships.

But aside from these, it is important to cultivate a personal relationship with God through prayer, reading the Bible, and seeking guidance from the Holy Spirit. This can provide the strength and wisdom needed to resist temptation and stay true to God's plan for purity and intimacy in relationships.

Building Emotional Intimacy and Connection

Building emotional intimacy and connection is essential in any relationship, including Christian dating. It's like building a house - you can't just throw up some walls and hope for the best. You need to put in the time and effort to make sure it's a sturdy foundation that will withstand the storms of life.

Emotional intimacy is the closeness that develops between two individuals as they share their thoughts, feelings, and experiences with each other. Emotional intimacy requires vulnerability and trust, and it can help create a healthy, solid and strong relationship. It's the kind of intimacy that allows you to be yourself, flaws and all, with your partner.

To build emotional intimacy and connection

Communicate openly and honestly with your partner. This means taking off the masks that we often wear to hide our true selves. Be willing to share your thoughts, feelings, and experiences with your partner, even if it's difficult or uncomfortable. It also involves listening actively to your partner, showing empathy and understanding, and being supportive. This means putting yourself in their shoes and seeing things from their point of view. Asking questions to clarify their thoughts and feelings and to make sure you're understanding them correctly can also be very helpful.

Spending quality time together also helps build emotional intimacy and connection. This could involve going on dates, engaging in shared hobbies or interests, or simply spending time talking and getting to know each other better. This means putting away distractions like phones and social media and being fully present with your partner. And hey, it doesn't always have to be an extravagant outing. Sometimes the most meaningful moments can be found in the simplest of activities.

Prayer is also a powerful tool for building emotional intimacy and connection. Praying together can create a sense of unity and trust, and it can also provide an opportunity to share personal struggles and concerns.

Overall, building emotional intimacy and connection requires intentional effort and a willingness to be vulnerable and honest with your partner. It can take time and patience, but at the long run, it is worth the effort to create a meaningful and strong relationship that can withstand any storm.

ACTION POINT

Reflect on your personal experiences with dating and how they have shaped your views so far.

Take home:

Seek accountability and support from a community of believers.

Chapter 8

PREPARING FOR MARRIAGE

Discerning God's Will in Your Relationship

As you embark on the journey of finding a life partner, you must ask yourself: are you merely seeking companionship, or are you seeking to discern God's divine will for your life? Discerning God's will is a crucial aspect of preparing for marriage. It involves seeking God's guidance and direction in the relationship and being open to his plan.

- *Pray for guidance* (James 1:5-6): Begin by praying and asking God for wisdom and guidance in your relationship. Ask Him to reveal His will to you and give you the discernment to recognize it.

- *Seek counsel* (Proverbs 15:22): Seek the counsel of wise and trusted mentors, pastors, and friends who have a strong foundation in the Word of God. Share your concerns and questions with them, and ask for their insights and advice. They can offer highly valued guidance and valuable insight based on their own experiences and knowledge of God's word.

- *Examine your motives*: Take an honest look at your motives for being in the relationship. Are you seeking to glorify God and build a Christ-centred partnership, or are you driven by your own desires and selfishness? Consider whether your motives align with God's will for your life.

- *Study the Scriptures* (Psalm 119:105): Spend time studying the Bible and seeking to understand God's principles for healthy relationships. Look for examples of godly relationships in the Bible, and seek to emulate those qualities in your own relationship.

- *Listen to the Holy Spirit* (John 16:13): Be open and attentive to the leading of the Holy Spirit. Pay attention to your intuition and any promptings or convictions you may feel. God often speaks to us through the Holy Spirit, so be willing to listen and obey.

- *Evaluate your compatibility*: Evaluate your compatibility with your partner in terms of your values, beliefs, goals, and vision for the future. Consider whether your partnership is helping you grow in your faith and draw closer to God.

- *Seek confirmation* (1 Thessalonians 5:21): Finally, seek confirmation from God through prayer, meditation, and reflection. Ask Him to confirm His will to you and give you the peace and confidence to move forward. This means being patient and waiting on God's timing, even if it's not what you want. It may also involve seeking signs or confirmation through circumstances or other means.

Discerning God's will is an ongoing process that requires patience, persistence, and faith. By following these steps and seeking the guidance of the Holy Spirit, you can find clarity and direction in your relationship and be confident in God's plan for your future.

Discerning God's will requires a willingness to submit to his plan and to trust in his goodness and faithfulness. It may involve making difficult decisions or sacrifices, but the reward -of being in alignment with God's will is a fulfilling and blessed marriage. God's plan is always perfect, and he knows what is best for us. As the Bible says in Jeremiah 29:11, *"For I know the plans I have for you," declares the Lord, "plans to prosper you and not to harm you, plans to give you hope and a future."* Building a strong and blessed marriage is not just about finding the right person, but also about aligning yourself with God's plan for your life.

As the Bible says in Proverbs 3:5-6, *"Trust in the Lord with all your heart and lean not on your own understanding; in all your ways submit to him, and he will make your paths straight."*

Understanding the Purpose of Engagement and courtship

Let's consider two scenarios: couple A that rushes into marriage without going through the intentional and purposeful stages of engagement and courtship. They may not have taken the time to discuss important topics such as finances, children, or spiritual goals, leaving their marriage vulnerable to potential conflicts and misunderstandings.

On the other hand, couple B that takes the time to intentionally prepare for marriage through engagement and courtship. They have open and honest communication, set healthy boundaries, seek wise counsel, and prioritize their relationship with God. This couple is more likely to have a strong foundation for a Christ-centred marriage that honours God and brings them joy and fulfilment.

Engagement and courtship are not just mere formalities or outdated traditions, but they serve a vital purpose in preparing couples for a lifetime commitment. The Bible speaks of the importance of building a strong foundation in Matthew 7:24-25, *"Therefore everyone who hears these words of mine and puts them into practice is like a wise man who built his house on the rock. The rain came down, the streams rose, and the winds blew and beat against that house; yet it did not fall, because it had its foundation on the rock."*

In Christendom, engagement and courtship are viewed as intentional and serious stages towards marriage. Courtship, is a period of getting to know each other better with the intention of discerning God's will for the relationship. During this time, the couple is encouraged to seek wise counsel from trusted mentors and family members. Courtship also involves setting healthy boundaries to ensure purity and emotional health in the relationship.

Engagement usually comes after the couple has decided to commit to each other and move towards marriage. The purpose of engagement is to prepare for the lifelong commitment of marriage by establishing a firm foundation in the relationship.

Both engagement and courtship are opportunities to prepare for a God-honouring marriage, and it is important to approach these stages with intentionality and prayerfulness. By seeking God's will and wisdom, couples can establish a strong foundation for a fulfilling and Christ-centred marriage.

During courtship, couples have the opportunity to grow deeper in their relationship and discern whether they are truly meant to spend the rest of their lives together. It is important for both individuals to have a clear understanding of the purpose and commitment of courtship.

Courtship and engagement period should focus on building a strong spiritual foundation. Couples should spend time praying together, reading the Bible, and discussing their faith and beliefs. It is important to ensure that both individuals are aligned in their values and vision for the future. It's not just about the bling on your finger or the Instagram likes, but about preparing yourself for a God-honouring marriage.

As Christians, seeking God's will and guidance is essential in preparing for marriage. This involves seeking wise counsel from mentors and leaders in the church and being open to the Holy Spirit's leading. It is important to have a humble and teachable spirit, as well as the willingness to surrender personal desires and plans to God's greater purpose.

Preparing for marriage also involves practical considerations such as financial management, developing communication skills, and conflict resolution. Engaged couples should take time to attend pre-marital counselling, workshops, and courses to help them build a strong foundation for their future marriage.

Engaging in intentional and prayerful engagement and courtship allows couples to build a strong foundation in their relationship that will help them weather any storm that comes their way. Through seeking God's will and wisdom, they can establish a firm Christ-centred foundation that will guide them through their marriage journey.

Premarital Counselling: Setting Your Marriage Up for Success

What is Premarital Counselling?

Premarital counselling is a type of counselling that couples receive before they get married. The goal is to help the couple understand each other better, build a strong foundation for their relationship, and prepare for the challenges of marriage. The counselling sessions can be conducted by a Christian counsellor, pastor, or minister, and can take place over several weeks or months.

During premarital counselling, couples are typically taught and opened to various aspects of marriage, including:

- *Communication skills:* Couples are taught how to communicate effectively and express their feelings, needs, and desires to each other. They learn active listening, conflict resolution, and how to avoid communication breakdowns.

- *Conflict resolution:* Couples are taught how to manage and resolve conflicts in a healthy manner. They learn how to identify the root causes of disagreements and how to find mutually beneficial solutions.

- *Financial management*: Couples are taught how to manage their finances together, create a budget, and plan for their financial future. They also learn how to handle financial disagreements.

- *Roles and expectations:* Couples are encouraged to openly discuss their roles and expectations in the marriage. This includes their individual roles, shared responsibilities, and expectations for the future.

- *Intimacy and sex*: Couples are taught about the importance of physical intimacy in marriage and how to maintain a healthy sexual relationship. They learn about sexual expectations, boundaries, and how to communicate their needs.

- *Family planning and parenting:* Couples are encouraged to discuss their plans for starting a family and their parenting styles. They learn how to handle the challenges that come with raising children, including balancing work and family life.

Premarital counselling is an essential part of preparing for a lifelong commitment in marriage. It provides couples with a safe and supportive space to address any issues, fears, or concerns that may arise during the engagement period. Investing in premarital counselling is a wise decision for any couple considering marriage. It helps prepare couples for a successful, fulfilling, and lasting marriage.

> **ACTION POINT**
>
> *Spend quality time in the place of prayer asking God to reveal His will for your marital life.*

Take home:

Seeking God's will is the key to a successful married life.

Chapter 9

ANSWERING COMMON QUESTIONS ABOUT DATING

What is the Purpose of Dating?

Dating is a thrilling adventure that every young person looks forward to. But as a Christian, dating should be more than just a casual fling. It should be to seek out a partner with whom you can build a God-centred and fulfilling relationship, leading to marriage. This involves getting to know someone on a deeper level, exploring shared values, goals, and interests, and discerning whether you are compatible and called by God to be together. As the Bible says in Amos 3:3, "Can two walk together, except they be agreed?"

It is important to remember that dating is not a game to be taken lightly, and should not be solely focused on physical attraction or personal pleasure. Instead, it should be approached with intentionality and with the ultimate goal of honouring God and pursuing His will for your life.

Dating can also serve as a time for personal growth and self-discovery, as you learn more about yourself and what you are looking for in a partner. By seeking God's guidance and being open to His plan, you can use the dating process as a way to deepen your faith and relationship with Him.

In the end, dating is a journey towards discovering God's purpose for your life. Trust in His plan, and He will guide you to the partner who will complement and enhance your journey towards a fulfilling and Christ-centred life together.

How Do I Know if This Person is the One?

As a Christian, discerning God's will and guidance is crucial in determining if someone is the one for you. It's important to seek God's guidance and understand

His plan for your life through praying, reading and meditating on His Word.

Also, it's important to consider whether the person shares your values, beliefs, and life goals. Are they committed to their faith? Do they have a strong character and integrity? Are you able to communicate openly and honestly with each other? These are all important factors to consider as you seek to discern whether someone is the one for you.

Consider seeking wise counsel from trusted Christian mentors or pastors. These individuals can offer guidance and support as you navigate the complexities of relationships and discern God's will for your life.

Seeking the one is not just about finding the right person, it's also about becoming the right person. Focus on personal growth and spiritual development, and trust in God's plan for your life. He will guide you to the right partner when the time is right.

How Far is Too Far?

When it comes to physical intimacy in a Christian dating relationship, it is important to set clear boundaries and adhere to them. While the Bible does not provide a specific list of physical actions that are allowed or prohibited, it does give guidance on the importance of sexual purity and avoiding sexual immorality. The Bible tells us in 1 Thessalonians 4:3-5, *"For this is the will of God, your sanctification: that you abstain from sexual immorality; that each one of you know how to control his own body in holiness and honour, not in the passion of lust like the Gentiles who do not know God."*

You both should have open and honest communication about your physical boundaries, taking into account your own personal convictions and the guidance of God's word. It is important to remember that physical intimacy is a gift from God that is meant to be enjoyed within the context of marriage.

As a general guideline, it is wise to avoid any physical activity that could lead to sexual arousal or temptation, such as prolonged kissing or intimate touching. Avoid being alone in private places which will compromise the set boundaries. It's easy to get caught up in the moment and let physical attraction take over.

In the end, the decision of how far is too far should be based on a desire to honour God and respect each other's purity and well-being. Prayerfully seek God's guidance and rely on the support of your community and accountability partners to help stay on track.

How do I Find a Godly Partner?

Finding a godly partner can be a challenging and sometimes daunting task, but the Almighty God, who created love and designed relationships, is more than able to lead you to your destined partner. One of the first steps in finding a godly partner is to prioritize your relationship with God. Seek to grow in your own faith and cultivate a deeper relationship with God through prayer, reading the bible, attending church, and joining a Christian community. This is a great way to meet like-minded people who share your faith.

Look for potential partners who share your values, beliefs, and priorities. This can be achieved by spending time with like-minded individuals, being intentional about meeting new people, and engaging in activities that align with your interests and values. Don't be afraid to ask questions about their faith and values, and seek to build a friendship before pursuing a romantic relationship.

Finding a godly partner is not solely up to you, but also requires trust in God's timing and plan for your life. Keep an open heart and mind, and trust that God will guide you to the right person.

How do I navigate Cultural Differences in Dating?

Dating a person who is from a different culture can be an exciting adventure, but it's not without its challenges. As a Christian, it's important to approach these differences with love and respect, just as Jesus would.

To navigate cultural differences in dating, start by learning about your partner's culture. Take the time to ask questions and understand their beliefs, values, and traditions. It's also important to be aware of your own cultural biases and to approach things with an open mind.

Remember that God created each of us uniquely, with our own cultural backgrounds and traditions. Embrace the beauty of diversity and seek to find common ground with your partner. When you respect and appreciate each other's differences, you can build a stronger, more vibrant relationship.

Communication is key in any relationship, but very essential when navigating cultural differences. Be open and honest about your expectations, boundaries, and any potential conflicts that may arise due to cultural differences and come up with solutions together. Avoid making assumptions or judgments based on your own cultural background. Instead, try to understand where your partner is coming from and find common ground.

Pray together and seek God's guidance as you work through these challenges.

As Christians, we are called to love and respect one another, regardless of our cultural backgrounds. In Galatians 3:28, it says, *"There is neither Jew nor Gentile, neither slave nor free, nor is there male and female, for you are all one in Christ Jesus."* Let this truth guide your approach to dating someone from a different culture, and trust that with God's help, you can build a strong relationship.

What practical steps can I take to balance my Personal Desires with God's Will?

Balancing personal desires with God's will can be a challenging process, but there are practical steps you can take to navigate this tension. Here are some suggestions:

1. **Spend time in prayer and bible study:** Seek God's guidance and wisdom through prayer and studying His word. This will help you discern His will for your life and align your desires with His.

2. **Seek wise counsel:** Surround yourself with trusted mentors and friends who can provide guidance and support as you navigate your dating journey. Seek counsel from those who have strong relationships with God and have experience in this area.

3. **Set healthy boundaries:** Establish clear boundaries and standards for your dating relationships, and stick to them. This will help you avoid compromising your values or falling into temptation.

4. **Prioritize personal growth:** Focus on becoming the person God created you to be. Invest in your own personal growth and development, and work to become the best version of yourself. This will not only help you attract a godly partner, but also prepare you for a healthy and fulfilling relationship.

5. **Trust in God's timing:** Remember that God's timing is perfect, even if it doesn't always align with our own desires. Trust in His plan for your life and be patient as you wait for the right person and the right relationship to come along.

By taking these practical steps, you can find a balance between your personal desires and God's will for your life, and ultimately pursue a relationship that honours God and brings joy and fulfilment to your life.

How do I handle disagreements with my partner in a Godly way?

Disagreements with your partner can be tough but can be handled in a godly way following a few key principles. Firstly, pray for wisdom and guidance from God, asking Him to give you the right words and actions to handle the situation in a way that honours Him.

Secondly, communicate openly and honestly with your partner, while also listening to their perspective with an open mind. Approach the situation with humility, seeking to understand rather than simply trying to prove your point.

You can also seek the advice and counsel of trusted Christian friends or mentors.

Above all, strive to approach the situation with love, grace, and a willingness to work together towards a resolution that is pleasing to God putting in mind the words of James 1:19-20: "*My dear brothers and sisters, take note of this: Everyone should be quick to listen, slow to speak and slow to become angry, because human anger does not produce the righteousness that God desires.*"

How do I deal with pressure from friends or family to date or marry someone who doesn't share my beliefs?

When facing pressure from friends or family to enter a romantic relationship or marriage with someone who doesn't share your faith, it can be quite challenging. There are however some steps you can take to handle the situation in a godly way.

First, it's important to stay true to your beliefs and values, even if it means going against the wishes of those around you. Pray for guidance and strength to make the right decision for your life, and trust that God has a plan for you.

Second, communicate openly and respectfully with your loved ones about your beliefs and why they are important to you. Try to find common ground and understanding, but also be firm in your convictions.

If the pressure becomes too overwhelming, seek support from other like-minded individuals, such as members of your church or a Christian support group. Surrounding yourself with a strong community can provide encouragement and accountability as you navigate these challenging situations.

In the Bible, we see examples of individuals who were faced with similar situations. One of them was Ruth, who chose to follow God and leave her family and country to be with Naomi (Ruth 1:16-17).

Despite the challenges she faced, God blessed her with a loving husband and a place in His family tree. In Daniel 3, we see Shadrach, Meshach, and Abednego refusing to worship a false idol, even when threatened with death. They knew that their allegiance was to God alone, and they were willing to face the consequences for their faith.

So take heart and trust in God's plan for your life, even when it's not the easiest path to take.

Your relationship with God should be your top priority, and it's important to make decisions that align with your faith and values. While it may be difficult to go against the wishes of your loved ones, ultimately, it's your life and your relationship with God that matters most.

How do I overcome past relationship baggage or trauma in order to have a healthy dating experience?

Here are some steps you can take:

1. **Acknowledge your past:** Recognize and accept that you have been hurt or experienced trauma in past relationships. It is important to

face your emotions and feelings head-on, rather than trying to ignore or suppress them.

2. **Seek help:** Consider seeking the help of a therapist or a trusted spiritual advisor who can provide guidance and support as you work through your past experiences. They can help you overcome negative thought patterns and behaviours.

3. **Practice self-care:** Take care of yourself physically, emotionally, and spiritually. Make time for activities that bring you joy and relaxation, such as exercising, praying, or spending time with loved ones.

4. **Focus on the present:** Instead of dwelling on the past, focus on the present moment and the potential for positive experiences in the future. This can include; setting new goals and aspirations for yourself, and learning to let go of negative thoughts and feelings that may be holding you back.

Remember that healing is a journey, and it takes time and effort. Be patient with yourself and seek support from those around you.

How do I maintain my individual identity and goals while still pursuing a relationship?

It's crucial to maintain your own identity and pursue your goals while still nurturing your relationship.

Some practical steps to take include:

1. **Set healthy boundaries:** Setting healthy boundaries is essential in any relationship. Establish clear boundaries around your time, priorities, and personal space. This will help you maintain a healthy balance between your personal goals and your relationship. When setting boundaries, communicate with your partner in a loving and respectful way.

2. **Pursue personal growth:** Don't neglect your personal growth and development in the pursuit of your relationship. Continue to invest in yourself and pursue your passions and interests. You are fearfully and wonderfully made by God, with unique talents, passions, and dreams, so don't let your relationship overshadow your own sense of purpose and direction. Bear in mind that God has a plan and purpose for your life,

and it's up to you to fulfil it. This will help you maintain a strong sense of identity and purpose, which can actually enhance your relationship.

3. **Support each other's goals:** Make sure to support each other in your individual goals and aspirations. Encourage your partner to pursue their passions and be their biggest cheerleader. A healthy relationship is built on mutual respect and support for each other's individual aspirations and goals.

4. **Have regular check-ins:** It's important to have regular check-ins with your partner to ensure that you're both still on the same page and moving in the same direction. Use this time to discuss your individual goals and priorities and how you can support each other in achieving them.

Don't hesitate to seek the guidance of a Christian counsellor or mentor if you need additional support in this area. A strong sense of self and purpose can actually enhance your relationship and make it even stronger. Embrace your individuality and work together with your partner to become the best version of yourselves. Proverbs 27:17 says *"As iron sharpens iron, so one person sharpens another."*

> **ACTION POINT**
>
> *Think of a challenging question about dating and bring it to a trusted mentor or pastor.*

> **Take home:**
>
> *It's okay to ask tough questions and seek guidance.*

Conclusion

Dear reader, as a follower of Christ, you are called to pursue relationships that glorify God and honour His design for love and marriage. Embracing God's plan for dating and relationships can be challenging, but it is ultimately rewarding. By focusing on spiritual and emotional intimacy, you can build deep connections with your partner that goes beyond physical attraction.

You must also learn to overcome past relationship wounds and guard your heart against negative influences. This involves setting healthy boundaries and seeking guidance and support from trusted mentors and friends. In doing so, you can prepare yourself for a fulfilling and long-lasting relationship.

Remember, dating is not just about finding the perfect partner, but also about becoming the best version of yourself. By committing to personal growth and seeking God's will in all aspects of your life, you can become the kind of person that attracts a loving and godly partner.

As you traverse the ups and downs of dating, you can take comfort in the fact that you are not alone. God is with you every step of the way, guiding and directing your paths. Whether you are single or in a relationship, your ultimate goal should always be to bring honour and glory to God.

So go forth with confidence and faith, knowing that God has a beautiful plan for your life and relationship.

May you seek His will and trust in His timing, knowing that He is faithful to fulfil His promises. May your dating and relationship be a testament to His love and grace, and may you always strive to put Him first in all that you do.

Final thoughts and words of wisdom

My dear young friend, as you embark on your journey towards a God-centred relationship, know that you are not alone. The path may not always be easy, but with God by your side, you can navigate the ups and downs with confidence and faith. Remember that *God's plan for your life and relationships is not to harm you, but to prosper and give you hope and a future (Jeremiah 29:11).*

So, as you enter into relationships, prioritize your relationship with God above all else. Seek His guidance and wisdom in your decisions and let Him lead you to a partner who shares your faith and values.

Communication is key in any relationship, and this is especially true in a God-centred relationship. Be open and honest with your partner about your beliefs, expectations, and boundaries. Remember that a relationship built on a foundation of honesty and trust will be much stronger than one built on secrets and deceit.

Set healthy boundaries to protect your heart and honour God in your relationship. This may mean avoiding certain behaviours or activities that do not align with your values.

Surround yourself with a community of believers who can offer guidance, support, and accountability as you navigate your relationship. Lean on them for encouragement and wisdom, and allow them to hold you accountable in areas where you may struggle.

Conclusion

May your journey towards a God-centred relationship be filled with grace, growth, and abundant blessings. And always remember, in Proverbs 3:5-6, *"Trust in the Lord with all your heart and lean not on your own understanding; in all your ways submit to him, and he will make your paths straight."*

Bibliography

- Adams, J. P. (2000). *Captivating the heart of God: A woman's ultimate pursuit.* Baker Books.

- Adams, J. P. (2011). *What makes a woman godly: Twenty crucial qualities every Christian woman should possess.* Baker Books. (Chapter 10: Choosing a Husband)

- Blackaby, H. T., & Blackaby, R. M. (2003). *Experiencing God at home.* Broadman & Holman Publishers. (Chapter 13: Praying for Your Future Spouse)

- Bridges, H. W. (2006). *Living on purpose: A biblical guide to a meaningful life.* NavPress. (Chapter 11: Choosing a Mate)

- Crabb, L. A. (2014). *Fully alive: A guide to emotional, physical, and spiritual intimacy.* Bethany House Publishers.

- Emerson, G. (2004). *The sanctity of marriage*. Broadman & Holman Publishers.

- Foster, J. H., & Foster, L. P. (2008). *The hidden option: Why every American needs a second date before the altar*. Simon and Schuster.

- Keener, C. S. (2005). *Women and men: Biblical principles for gender roles*. Baker Academic.

- Smalley, G., & Smalley, N. (2003). *Love is a decision: The 5 secrets to lasting love in marriage*. Zondervan.

- Smalley, G., & Smalley, N. (2004). *For better and for always: A couple's guide to lasting love*. Zondervan.

- Warren, R. (2012). *The purpose driven life: What on Earth am I here for?* Zondervan. (Chapter 31: Praying for Your Future Spouse)

- White, J. M. (2017). *A heart that can break: Why God leads us to love and loss*. Thomas Nelson.

Other Books by the Author

1. Help My Heart.
2. Pathways to unlimited Joy.
3. Joyful Living 30-Day Journal.
4. Exchanging My Disabilities for God's Ability
5. A Child's Guide to Prayer.
6. Colouring and Activities Prayer Book.
7. A Prayer Guide for Parents and Grandparents.
8. Joy Comes in the Morning Bible Study Journal.
9. Joyful Reflections Journal: A Personal Guide to Study the Bible in 6 Months.
10. Joyful Reflections: A Sermon Notebook for Personal and Spiritual Growth.
11. Joy Comes in the Morning: Strategies for finding joy in every area of life.

Other Books by the Author

12. The Joyful Authors Blueprint: 7 proven steps to write and launch your book in 90 days
13. The Joyful Authors Workbook.
14. The Family's Secret
15. 2024 Joyful Living Diary
16. Joyful Living Diary
17. Joyful Daily Reflections: A Personal Guide to Study the Bible in One Year.

www.ingramcontent.com/pod-product-compliance
Lightning Source LLC
Chambersburg PA
CBHW032001080426
42735CB00007B/477